BORDERLINE
CAUSES, INFLUENCE AND THERAPY

I0768296

Introduction: What is Borderline ?

Introduction: What is Borderline ? Borderline or Borderline Personality Disorder (BPD) is a mental illness characterized by persistent instability in mood, self-image, behavior and interpersonal relationships. People with borderline can often behave very impulsively, have difficulty regulating their emotions and tend to have extremely intense and unstable interpersonal relationships. Symptoms of borderline include severe mood swings, impulsivity, self-injurious behavior, chronic feelings of emptiness, identity insecurity, intense and unstable interpersonal relationships and often a strong sense of abandonment. The symptoms can manifest themselves in different forms and can be different for each person. There are various therapeutic approaches for borderline, which aim to improve emotional regulation and stabilize interpersonal relationships. Therapy can include a combination of psychotherapy, medication and self-help measures.

The history of borderline personality disorder

Borderline personality disorder (BPD) was first described in the 1930s by psychoanalysts treating patients with severe emotional instability. The term "borderline" refers to the fact that these patients appeared to be on the borderline between neurosis and psychosis. In the 1970s, researchers recognized BPD as a disorder in its own right and began to study it as a clinical syndrome. The symptoms of BPD, such as unstable mood, relationships and self-image, were better understood and more effective treatments were developed. In the 1980s, BPD was included as an official mental disorder in the Diagnostic and Statistical Manual of Mental Disorders (DSM), which is a diagnostic classification system for mental disorders. Since then, research on BPD has evolved and there are a variety of treatment options, including psychotherapy, medication and Dialectical Behavioral Therapy (DBT). However, there is also criticism of the diagnosis of BPD, as some experts argue that the symptoms of the disorder are too non-specific and overlap with other mental disorders. There is also controversy over the causes of BPD, including whether it is a biological or psychosocial disorder, or whether it is a mixture of both. Despite these controversies, BPD remains an important mental disorder that affects many people, and research and treatment of the disorder continues.

Borderline personality disorder

(BPD) is usually diagnosed by a qualified psychiatrist or psychologist. The diagnosis is based on a thorough clinical examination and an assessment of symptoms and signs. The diagnosis of BPD requires that at least five of the following symptoms or behaviors occur over a period of more than one year. Intense mood swings that are : ten disproportionate to the situation. Problems with impulse control, such as risky behaviors or substance abuse. Difficulties with interpersonal relationships, including unstable and intense relationships and alternating between idealizing and devaluing others. Low self-esteem and identity insecurity. Recurrent suicidal thoughts, suicide attempts or self-harming behavior. Feelings of emptiness or boredom. Irritability and outbursts of anger. It is also important to rule out other disorders that may have similar symptoms, such as bipolar disorder, depression, anxiety disorders or post traumatic stress disorder. The-diagnosis of BPD can be complex as it is a multi-faceted disorder that affects different areas of life. It is important that the diagnosis is made by a qualified professional who has experience in the diagnosis and treatment of BPD. The symptoms of personality disorde (BPD) is a mental illness characterized by unstable mood, relationships and behaviors. There are many symptoms of borderline that can affect different aspects of life. People with BPD may experience frequent and intense mood swings that can occur within hours or days. They may feel happy and energetic, only to suddenly become sad and empty.Impulsive behavior is another symptom of borderline. This can manifest itself through uncontrolled outbursts of anger, risky behavior (such as substance abuse or speeding), eating disorders or self-harm. Unstable relationships: People with borderline often have difficulty maintaining close relationships. They may form a strong emotional attachment to someone, only to suddenly drop it or leave out of fear of rejection. Identity disorder: A person with borderline may have difficulty defining their identity or self-image. They may feel that they have no clear idea of who they are or what they want in life. People with borderline may suf er from severe anxiety and depression symptoms. They may feel that they are unable to control their emotions or behavior, leading to feelings of hopelessness and isolation. Paranoia: Some people with borderline may show signs of paranoia, such as feeling that others are against them or persecuting them. People with Borderline often have a very strong fear of abandonment. This fear can be so strong that they will go to great lengths to maintain their relationships, even if it is to their own detriment. Self-harming behavior: Self-injurious behavior, such as cutting or burning one's own skin, is a common symptom of borderline. It can serve as a coping mechanism to relieve emotional pain. Suicidal thoughts and attempts: People with borderline have an increased risk of suicidal thoughts and attempts. It is important to take these symptoms seriously and seek professional help if you or someone you know exhibits these symptoms. Emotional instability: Borderline can lead to a general instability of emotions. People with BPD can often feel that their emotions are out of control and difficult to manage. Stress-induced perceptual distortions: People with borderline may have distorted perceptions in stressful situations. For example, they may believe that others are accusing them of evil intentions.

Borderline and self-harm

Borderline is a personality disorder characterized by impulsivity, unstable emotions, relationships and identity. People with borderline often have difficulty dealing with their feelings and may self-harm in order to calm down or control their emotions. Self-harm is a common side effect of borderline. It is important to note that self-harm is not a suicide attempt. It is a form of coping with emotions and can help to temporarily relieve pain. Self-harm can take many forms, such as cutting, burning, scratching or hitting. It can be difficult to understand the reasons behind the behavior, as it is often linked to feelings of shame and guilt. It is important to note that borderline and self-harm are not the same thing and not everyone who suffers from borderline self-harm. However, it is important to understand that self-harm can be part of the clinical picture and is a form of coping with emotions. People with borderline often experience severe mood swings and have difficulty controlling their emotions. They can move quickly from happiness to sadness or anger and have difficulty focusing on a particular emotion. The unstable emotions can lead to conflict in relationships and can make it difficult to maintain a healthy relationship. People with borderline can also have difficulty finding their identity. They can quickly fall in love with relationships, but also quickly lose interest in them. They may also have difficulty defining their career goals and can often feel uncertain about their future. There are treatment options for borderline and self-harm, which often include a combination of therapy and medication. Therapy can help manage emotional instability and learn emotion regulation techniques. Medication can help to reduce mood swings and depression. If you are affected yourself or know someone who is affected by borderline or self-harm, it is important to seek support. There are many resources available, such as therapists, support groups and hotlines. It is also important to note that it is not helpful to judge or stigmatize someone affected by borderline or self-injury. It is important to show compassion and understanding and to recognize that these disorders require medical treatment. Overall, borderline is a serious disorder that can severely affect people's quality of life. Self-harm is a form of coping with emotions and can be part of the clinical picture.

Borderline and suicide

Borderline and suicide are two topics that are closely linked. Borderline personality disorder is characterized by instability in mood, behavior, identity and interpersonal relationships. This can lead to unpredictable, intense and sometimes self-destructive behaviors. Suicide is a result of these self-destructive tendencies and can be a very real danger for people with borderline personality disorder. People with borderline personality disorder often have a deep sense of emptiness that drives them to self-destructive acts. These actions can take the form of eating disorders, substance abuse, self-injurious behavior and suicidal thoughts and attempts. They can also include impulsive behavior and inappropriate reactions to everyday situations. Suicidal thoughts and attempts are very common in people with borderline personality disorder. In fact, up to 70% of people with borderline personality disorder have suicidal thoughts or attempts at some point in their lives. The reasons for this are varied and can range from severe emotional pain to a feeling that life is simply not worth living. It is important to understand that suicidal thoughts and attempts are not just a whim or a cry for attention. They are a serious mental illness and should not be taken lightly. It is also important to note that people with borderline personality disorder often try to hide or minimize their suicidal thoughts or attempts for fear of stigma or rejection. If you know someone who is experiencing suicidal thoughts or is in crisis, it is important that you act quickly and seek professional help. This may include contacting a crisis hotline, a mental health clinic or a therapist. If you are in crisis yourself, you should reach out to one of the resources mentioned above or reach out to a trusted friend or family member. There are also some steps that people with borderline personality disorder can take to reduce their suicidal thoughts and attempts. These include: Seeking professional help: Seeking treatment from a psychiatrist or therapist can help reduce the symptoms of borderline personality disorder and develop strategies for coping with suicidal thoughts. Seek support: It can be helpful to join a support group or a group of people with similar experiences for support and understanding. Coping with stress: It is important to find ways to cope with stress and identify emotional triggers.

What causes borderline?

Borderline personality disorder (BPD) is a mental illness characterized by unstable moods, interpersonal relationships and self-image. There is no clear cause for borderline, but it is thought that a combination of biological, genetic and environmental factors may contribute. Biological factors: Some studies have shown that there is a link between borderline and biological factors such as brain chemistry. Neurotransmitters such as serotonin and noradrenaline can influence how people process and regulate emotions. Research has shown that people with borderline personality disorder may experience changes in the function of these neurotransmitters in the brain. Genetic factors: There is also evidence that borderline personality disorder can run in families. Studies have shown that people whose family members also suffer from borderline personality disorder have a higher risk of developing the disorder themselves. However, it is important to note that genetics is only part of the picture and that environmental factors can also play an important role.Environmental factors such as traumatic experiences can Environmental factors: contribute to the development of borderline personality disorder. It has been shown that people who have experienced traumatic events such as abuse, neglect or separation in childhood have a higher risk of developing borderline personality disorder later in life. Difficult family circumstances such as divorce or the loss of a parent can also contribute to this. Another important role is played by interpersonal relationships, especially in childhood. People who did not have stable and secure relationships in childhood may have difficulty building trust and self-regulating, which can lead to symptoms of borderline.Personal factors such as temperament and personality ca Personal factors: n also contribute to the development of borderline. People with an impulsive or unstable temperament may be more prone to borderline. Similarly, people with a personality characterized by a poor ability to regulate emotions or difficulty coping with stress may be at a higher risk of developing borderline. Treatment: There is no cure for borderline, but there are treatments that can help alleviate the symptoms. One of the most effective treatments is Dialectical Behavioral Therapy (DBT), which focuses on improving emotional regulation, interpersonal skills and mindfulness. Other treatment options may include antidepressants, antipsychotics and anti-anxiety medications.

Genetics and borderline

Borderline personality disorder (BPD) is a psychiatric disorder characterized by unstable emotions, interpersonal relationships and self-perception. The genetic factors that contribute to the development of BPD are not yet fully understood, but there is evidence that genetic predisposition plays a role. Twin studies have shown that BPD is more common in identical twins than in fraternal twins, suggesting that genes may play a role. Some researchers have identified specific genes that have been linked to BPD, including the serotonin transporter gene (SLC6A4) and the monoamine oxidase A gene (MAOA). The SLC6A4 gene codes for a transporter that removes serotonin from the synaptic cleft, while the MAOA gene codes for an enzyme that breaks down neurotransmitters such as serotonin and dopamine. There is evidence that certain variants of these genes may be associated with an increased risk of BPD. There is also evidence that epigenetic changes, such as DNA methylation, may play a role in BPD. DNA methylation is a form of gene regulation in which methyl groups are attached to DNA to influence gene expression. Studies have shown that certain genes may be methylated differently in people with BPD compared to people without BPD. Although the exact genetic factors that contribute to the development of BPD are not yet fully understood, it is important to note that genetics is only part of the story. BPD is influenced by a variety of factors, including trauma, environmental factors and psychological factors. Another interesting aspect of genetics and BPD is the possibility of genetic testing to predict a person's risk for developing BPD. Although no such tests currently exist, researchers are striving to identify specific genes or combinations of genes that are associated with an increased risk of BPD. However, it is important to note that genetic testing alone does not provide a complete diagnosis of BPD and that it must be used in combination with other diagnostic tools and clinical assessments. Overall, research shows that genetics can play a role in the development of BPD, but it is important to note that this is only part of the story and that other factors also play an important role. However, a deeper understanding of the genetic factors that contribute to the development of BPD could help to develop better diagnosis and treatment options to alleviate the suffering of affected individuals.

Environmental factors and borderline

Borderline personality disorder (BPD) is a mental illness characterized by impulsivity, instability in interpersonal relationships, mood swings and identity disturbances. Although the cause of this disorder is not fully understood, experts believe that environmental factors may play an important role in its development. There are several environmental factors that have been linked to an increased risk of developing BPD, including trauma, abuse and neglect in childhood. Children who are exposed to abuse or neglect are at increased risk for a variety of mental disorders, including BPD. Traumatic events in childhood can also contribute to poor emotional regulation, which is commonly observed in people with BPD. Another important environmental factor associated with BPD is unstable or traumatic interpersonal relationships. People with BPD often have difficulty maintaining stable and supportive relationships. If they grow up in an environment where interpersonal relationships are unstable or traumatic, this can affect their ability to build and maintain healthy relationships. Family environmental factors can also play a role in the development of BPD. People with BPD often have a difficult family history, including family members with mental disorders or addictions. A family with unstable relationships or high rates of conflict can also increase the risk of developing BPD. There are also other environmental factors associated with BPD, such as the loss of a loved one, experiencing abandonment or pressure to act in a certain way. These factors can contribute to the inability of people with BPD to effectively regulate their emotions and cause them to react impulsively. Although environmental factors can play an important role in the development of BPD, it is important to emphasize that not all people who experience traumatic events or unstable relationships automatically develop BPD. It is also possible that genetic factors may play a role in the development of BPD, although this is not fully understood. Overall, it is important to emphasize that BPD is a complex disorder and there is no simple explanation for its development. A combination of biological, psychological and environmental factors can contribute to a person developing BPD. If you believe that you or someone you know has BPD, it is important to seek professional help to get an accurate diagnosis and receive appropriate treatment.

Borderline and trauma

Borderline is a personality disorder characterized by instability in mood, behavior and interpersonal relationships. Trauma refers to an experience that a person perceives as threatening or dangerous and that causes an intense emotional reaction. People with borderline personality disorder often also have a history of trauma. However, it is important to note that not all people with borderline have a history of trauma and not all people with a history of trauma have borderline personality disorder. Trauma can occur in many ways, including physical, sexual or emotional abuse, neglect, or witnessing violence or death. People with a history of trauma may also suffer from post-traumatic stress disorder (PTSD), which is characterized by uncontrollable anxiety, re-experiencing of traumatic events, avoidance behaviors, and excessive reactions to certain stimuli. People with borderline personality disorder often have difficulty regulating their emotions and may exhibit severe mood swings, impulsive behavior and self-harm disorders. They may also have problems maintaining interpersonal relationships and tend to move from one person to another or be in relationships characterized by instability and conflict. The effects of trauma on people with borderline personality disorder can be severe and can lead to the symptoms of the disorder being exacerbated. Trauma can also contribute to people with borderline personality disorder self-harming in order to regulate their emotions or avoid negative memories. Treating borderline personality disorder and trauma can be a complex challenge. Therapies such as Dialectical Behavioral Therapy (DBT) and Cognitive Behavioral Therapy (CBT) have been shown to be effective in treating borderline symptoms. However, it can be difficult for people with trauma to engage in therapy as it can be very difficult to talk about traumatic events.

One type of therapy that has been shown to be effective in treating borderline personality disorder and trauma is Trauma-Focused Cognitive Behavioral Therapy (TF-CBT). This therapy helps people process their traumatic experiences by identifying their negative thoughts and feelings and then developing new, positive thoughts and beliefs that help them process and recover from their experiences. Medication can also be used in the treatment of borderline personality disorder and trauma.

Borderline and abuse

Borderline is a personality disorder characterized by unstable moods, relationships and self-images. People with borderline often have difficulty regulating their emotions, which can lead to impulsive behavior. They may also have difficulty defining themselves and often have a fear of abandonment. When it comes to abuse, there are many different forms, including physical, sexual, emotional and psychological abuse. Abuse can have serious effects on victims, including traumatic experiences, loss of self-esteem and long-term mental health problems. People with borderline may be at higher risk of experiencing abuse due to their instability and difficulties with emotion regulation. In some cases, people with borderline may also unknowingly contribute to abuse by getting into unhealthy relationships or putting themselves in dangerous situations. One way that Borderline and abuse can be related is through the relationship between the abuser and the victim. People with borderline may be more vulnerable to relationships with abusers due to their fear of abandonment and instability. Abusers may take advantage of a person with borderline's need for emotional closeness and validation and present themselves as a savior to control the relationship and manipulate the victim. In some cases, abuse can also cause a person to develop borderline personality disorder. Traumatic experiences can lead to emotional instability, which can cause people to have difficulty regulating their emotions and maintaining healthy relationships. It is important to note that not all people with Borderline are abused, and not all victims of abuse develop Borderline Personality Disorder. Each person is unique and the way they respond to traumatic experiences can vary greatly. If someone is struggling with borderline or abusive experiences, it is important that they seek professional help. Psychotherapy can help improve emotion regulation, boost self-esteem and build healthy relationships. There are also support groups for people with borderline and victims of abuse that can provide a supportive community. In terms of the relationship between borderline and abuse, it is important that people with borderline learn to build and maintain healthy relationships. Learning emotion regulation and self-esteem building skills can help them feel safer in relationships and better able to recognize and avoid abuse. If you or someone you know has been affected by abuse.

Borderline and family

Borderline personality disorder (BPD) is a mental illness that can severely affect the daily lives of those affected as well as the lives of their family members. In this text, I will take a closer look at the impact of BPD on families and explain how family members can cope with this disorder. First of all, it is important to understand what borderline is and how it manifests itself. Borderline is a disorder characterized by severe mood swings, impulsivity, unstable relationships and a disturbed self-image. Those affected may have difficulty regulating their emotions and may self-harm or have suicidal thoughts in extreme situations. These symptoms can put a great strain on family life, as family members often do not know how to deal with the unpredictable and intense mood swings. Family members can often feel helpless when trying to cope with a BPD member. They may feel overwhelmed, overwhelming and isolated if they don't know how to respond to certain behaviors or outbursts. It is important that family members understand that BPD is an illness and that the person's behavior is not necessarily caused by their personality or character. There are many things family members can do to deal with Borderline and keep family life as normal as possible. One of the most important things is to set boundaries. It is important to set clear boundaries for the BPD member's behavior and to enforce these boundaries consistently. In this way, family life can be protected from unpredictable mood swings. Family members can also try to offer support to the BPD member in seeking professional help. Therapy can help the sufferer learn to regulate their emotions and manage their impulses. Therapy can also help the sufferer to develop a stronger sense of self-worth and thus be able to have more stable relationships. It is also important that family members take care of their own health. They should take time for themselves and respect their own needs and boundaries. Family members can also turn to a support group or counseling center for support and advice from other family members in similar situations. Overall, it is important that family members understand that borderline is a disorder and that the BPD member's behavior is not always controllable. It is important to set boundaries, offer professional help and take care of your own health.

Borderline and friendships

Borderline is a personality disorder characterized by an unstable mood, impulsive behavior, intense interpersonal relationships and a disturbed self-image. This disorder can make it difficult for people with borderline to maintain or nurture friendships. In this article, we will take a closer look at borderline and friendships. One of the challenges for people with Borderline when it comes to friendships is that they often rush in and out of a relationship quickly. This quick volatility can be difficult for friends to understand and cope with. It can also cause people with borderline to struggle to build trust and feel secure in the relationship. For this reason, it can be difficult for people with Borderline to maintain close and long-term friendships. Another characteristic of borderline is that people with this disorder often react very emotionally and can be easily hurt. This can lead them to easily blame or accuse their friends of abandoning them or intentionally hurting them. This type of behavior can make friends feel uncomfortable and withdraw. However, friendships can also play a positive role in the lives of people with borderline. A good friendship can be an important support in dealing with the emotional challenges that this disorder can bring. A friend can also help people to connect with others and feel less isolated. However, when people with borderline try to maintain a friendship, there are some things they should keep in mind. For example, it can be helpful to be aware of how they behave in the relationship and how this may affect their friend. It can also be useful to have open and honest conversations about the challenges associated with borderline and how this may affect the friendship. Through this open communication, misunderstandings can be avoided and trust can be strengthened. Another important aspect is that people with borderline often experience intense emotions. When they share these emotions, it can be difficult for friends to deal with them or respond appropriately. In these moments, it is important that people with borderline learn how to regulate their emotions and how to help friends better understand their reactions. One way to do this is through mindfulness exercises or emotional regulation techniques such as breathing exercises or progressive muscle relaxation. Finally, it can also be helpful to seek support from a therapist who specializes in borderline. A therapist can help to better understand the challenges of maintaining friendships and provide techniques and tools.

Borderline and romantic relationships

Borderline personality disorder (BPD) is a mental illness characterized by intense emotions, impulsive behavior, and unstable interpersonal relationships. Being in a romantic relationship with someone who has BPD can be both challenging and rewarding. In this article, we will look at the challenges and potential benefits of a romantic relationship with someone with BPD. The challenges instability of emotions: People with BPD often have intense and unpredictable emotions. In a romantic relationship, this can mean that the partner is often unexpectedly overwhelmed by anger, sadness or joy. This can be difficult to deal with, especially if the partner is not emotionally unstable themselves. Impulsivity: People with BPD tend to act impulsively. This can mean that they do things without thinking about them or considering the consequences. In a romantic relationship, this may mean that the partner engages in risky or unhealthy behaviors, such as drug use or risky sexual encounters. Fear of abandonment: People with BPD often have a fear of abandonment. This can mean that they become clingy in the relationship and overly possessive or jealous. It can also mean that they accuse their partner of abandoning them, even when this is not the case. Difficulty setting boundaries: People with BPD often have difficulty setting boundaries. In a romantic relationship, this can mean that they overly seek attention or love and feel vulnerable if they don't get the response they want. It can also mean that they don't respect their partner when they set boundaries. The potential benefits Intensity and passion: People with BPD often have a deeply felt emotion and passion. In a romantic relationship, this can mean that the partner feels loved and desired, as the love and affection coming from the person with BPD can be very intense. Empathy: People with BPD are often very sensitive and can empathize with the feelings of others. In a romantic relationship, this can mean that the partner feels understood and supported. Creativity: People with BPD often have a creative and artistic streak. In a romantic relationship, this can mean that the partner can benefit from the creativity and inspiration of the person with BPD. Deep connection: People with BPD tend to take relationships very seriously and identify strongly with their partner. In a romantic relationship, this can mean that the partner develops a deep emotional connection with the person with BPD.

Borderline and work

Borderline personality disorder is a mental illness characterized by unstable moods, relationships and self-images. People with borderline can have difficulty regulating their emotions and may experience extreme mood swings, impulsive behavior and problems with interpersonal communication. This can also have an impact on their ability to find and keep work. For people with Borderline, finding work can be particularly difficult as they may have problems with interpersonal relationships and have difficulty controlling their emotions in the workplace. They may also have difficulty focusing on tasks and maintaining their energy, which can lead to performance issues. However, there are also many people with borderline who are successful in their jobs and can successfully manage their symptoms. Here are some ways that people with Borderline can succeed in their careers: Get support: it can be helpful to seek therapy or counseling to help you manage your borderline symptoms and learn how to deal with work stress. Supportive therapy can also help to boost self-esteem and improve interpersonal skills. Find a supportive work environment: It can be helpful to look for a job that offers a supportive environment where you can develop and contribute your skills and abilities. A positive work environment can help reduce stress and improve your ability to self-regulate. Use flexible working arrangements: For people with Borderline, flexible working arrangements such as telecommuting or working time agreements can be a useful way to manage their workload and manage their symptoms. It can also be helpful to take breaks from work to recuperate and focus on your work. Work on your interpersonal skills: People with borderline often have difficulty regulating their emotions and maintaining interpersonal relationships. It can be helpful to work on these skills and learn how to communicate effectively and resolve conflicts. Create a good work-life balance: It is important to maintain a good work-life balance to manage your symptoms and keep your energy up. Schedule time for self-care and relaxation and try to keep work and leisure separate. In some cases, it may also be necessary to take out disability insurance (DI). People with borderline may have difficulty holding down a full-time job, and disability insurance can help provide financial support.

Borderline and therapy

Borderline personality disorder (BPD) is a mental illness characterized by unstable moods, interpersonal relationships and self-image. It is a serious disorder that can severely affect the lives of those affected. Borderline personality disorder is usually diagnosed after an extensive clinical interview and review of the patient's medical history. Treatment for borderline personality disorder usually involves a combination of psychotherapy, medication and supportive measures. Psychotherapy is the first choice in the treatment of borderline personality disorder. Dialectical Behavioral Therapy (DBT) is a specialized form of psychotherapy developed specifically for the treatment of borderline personality disorder. DBT has proven to be very effective and is the most commonly recommended therapy for BPD. DBT is based on four core areas that aim to reduce the emotional dysregulations faced by BPD patients. These core areas include: Mindfulness: the ability to be present in the present moment and consciously focus attention on what is happening in the moment without judging or evaluating it. Emotion regulation: The ability to recognize, understand and regulate emotions. This includes identifying emotional triggers and using techniques to reduce emotional intensity and duration. Interpersonal Skills: The ability to build and maintain effective and healthy relationships. This includes developing communication skills and the ability to resolve conflict. Crisis management: The ability to deal with stressful situations and crises without engaging in self-harming behavior. Medication can also play an important role in the treatment of borderline personality disorder. Antidepressants and antipsychotics can be used in the treatment of depression, anxiety and other psychological symptoms that often accompany BPD. However, it is important to note that medication alone is not an effective treatment for BPD and should always be used in conjunction with psychotherapy. Supportive measures can also play an important role in the treatment of borderline personality disorder. These can include self-help groups, support from friends and family and other activities to promote well-being and relaxation.

The different types of therapy for borderline

Borderline personality disorder is a mental illness characterized by unstable mood, interpersonal relationships and a disturbed self-image. People with this disorder often have difficulty regulating their emotions and maintaining their relationships with other people. There are various types of therapies that can help people with borderline personality disorder to alleviate their symptoms and improve their lives. Some of these therapies are described below. Dialectical Behavior Therapy (DBT) DBT is one of the most commonly used forms of therapy for borderline personality disorder. It is a type of cognitive behavioral therapy that aims to improve the patient's emotion regulation and interpersonal skills. DBT is based on the assumption that people with borderline personality disorder have difficulty regulating their emotions and therefore often act impulsively. Therapy often involves individual and group sessions in which patients learn emotion regulation techniques and how to improve their interpersonal relationships. Schema-Focused Therapy (SFT) SFT is a form of psychotherapy that aims to improve the patient's disturbed self-image and relationships with other people. Therapy often involves individual sessions in which patients learn how to identify and change their negative beliefs and behavior patterns. The therapy is long-term and can last for months or even years. Transference-Focused Psychotherapy (TFP) TFP is a type of psychoanalysis that focuses on the transference process between the patient and the therapist. The therapy often involves weekly sessions in which the therapist talks to the patient about their interpersonal relationships and how they can improve them. The therapy is based on the assumption that patients often have negative transfers to their interpersonal relationships and that these transfers can be examined and worked on in therapy. Mentalization-based therapy (MBT) MBT is a form of psychotherapy based on the assumption that people with borderline personality disorder have difficulty understanding other people's thoughts and emotions. Therapy often involves individual and group sessions in which patients learn to recognize and understand their own and other people's thoughts and emotions. Therapy can also aim to improve patients' interpersonal skills and relationships.

Dialectical-behavioral therapy (DBT)

Dialectical Behavioral Therapy (DBT) is a form of psychotherapy that was developed specifically for people with Borderline Personality Disorder (BPD). However, it has now also established itself as an effective treatment method for a range of other mental disorders. The aim of DBT is to help patients improve their emotion regulation, strengthen their interpersonal relationships and increase their ability to cope with stressful situations. DBT is based on an integrative approach that combines elements from different therapeutic schools such as behavioral therapy, cognitive therapy, Zen meditation and mindfulness practice. A central aspect of DBT is the acceptance and validation of the patient's emotions. Therapists encourage patients to accept and embrace their feelings without judging or evaluating them. This approach enables patients to understand themselves better and to regulate their emotions in a targeted manner. Another important component of DBT is the training of skills for emotion regulation, interpersonal communication and stress management. Patients learn to identify their feelings, regulate their emotions and improve their interpersonal relationships. In addition, techniques for coping with stressful situations are taught in order to avoid relapses and crises. Another feature of DBT is the concept of dialectics. This refers to the ability to accept and hold two seemingly contradictory ideas or concepts at the same time. In DBT, this means that patients learn to accept their own experience and emotions while accepting and respecting the perspective of others. This ability to be dialectical is particularly important for people with borderline personality disorder, as they often tend to think and act in extremes. DBT is usually conducted in group therapy sessions led by an experienced therapist. The groups provide patients with a supportive and structured environment in which they can share their experiences and learn from others. In addition, individual therapy sessions and telephone coaching sessions can be offered to provide patients with individualized support. DBT has been shown to be an effective treatment method for a range of mental disorders, including borderline personality disorder, chronic depression, post-traumatic stress disorder, eating disorders and substance abuse. Studies have shown that DBT can reduce the symptoms of these disorders and improve patients' quality of life.

Cognitive behavioral therapy (CBT)

Cognitive behavioral therapy (CBT) is one of the most commonly used forms of psychotherapy. It is designed to identify and change patterns of behavior and thinking that can have a negative impact on a person's emotional health and well-being. The basics and methods of cognitive behavioral therapy are explained below. Basics of cognitive behavioral therapy Cognitive behavioral therapy assumes that our thoughts, feelings and behaviors are interconnected and influence each other. Negative thought patterns can lead to negative emotions and behaviors, which in turn can reinforce our thoughts. The goal of CBT is to identify these negative thought patterns and replace them with positive, constructive thoughts that lead to positive emotions and behaviors. Methods of cognitive behavioral therapy Cognitive restructuring An important method of CBT is cognitive restructuring. This involves identifying negative thought patterns and replacing them with positive, constructive thoughts. The person is instructed to question their negative thoughts and check whether they are really true and helpful. If not, alternative thoughts are developed to help the person think more positively and feel better. Behavioral experiments Another important method of CBT is behavioral experiments. This involves identifying negative behaviors and replacing them with positive behaviors. The person is encouraged to try out new behaviors and see how they affect their thoughts and feelings. This can help to break negative behavior patterns and establish new, positive behavior patterns. Exposure therapy Exposure therapy is a method used to treat anxiety disorders and post-traumatic stress disorder. The person is gradually confronted with the things or situations that trigger their anxiety in order to reduce their anxiety reactions. The person learns that their anxiety reactions decrease when they face the fear instead of avoiding it. Relaxation exercises Relaxation exercises such as progressive muscle relaxation or breathing exercises can help to reduce physical tension and stress. By learning to relax, the person can better control their negative thoughts and emotions and think more positively. Problem-solving strategies CBT can also help to develop problem-solving strategies to cope better with difficult situations.

Psychoanalysis and borderline

Borderline personality disorder (BPD) is a severe mental illness characterized by unstable moods, relationships and impulse control. The causes of BPD are not yet fully understood, but many researchers believe that a combination of biological, psychological and environmental factors play a role. Psychoanalysis is a form of psychotherapy based on the ideas of Sigmund Freud. Freud believed that the causes of psychological disorders lie in the unconscious and that treatment consists of uncovering and working on unconscious conflicts. Although psychoanalysis is no longer as widely used as it once was, some therapists still have success treating borderline patients. In psychoanalysis, the relationship between therapist and patient is seen as central. The therapist should establish a safe and stable relationship with the patient that enables the patient to uncover and work through their inner conflicts. Borderline patients often have difficulty maintaining stable relationships and may have difficulty establishing a secure relationship in therapy. Some psychoanalysts believe that borderline patients develop a special kind of transference in therapy. Transference is a psychological concept that describes how the patient transfers their experiences with other people to the therapist. In psychoanalysis, transference is seen as an important source of information about the patient's inner conflicts. Some psychoanalysts believe that borderline patients develop a type of transference known as "borderline transference". This transference is characterized by an extreme intensity of the relationship with the therapist and a tendency to idealize or devalue the therapist. Borderline patients may also have difficulty accepting boundaries and may see the therapist as a substitute for a missing parental figure. Working on borderline transference is an important component of psychoanalysis with borderline patients. The therapist must be able to recognize and understand the patient's transference in order to help the patient uncover and work through their inner conflicts. The therapist must also be able to set clear boundaries and maintain a safe therapeutic relationship. Another concept that is important in psychoanalysis for borderline patients is the concept of the self. The self is the central concept of identity and refers to what a person perceives themselves to be. Borderline patients often have difficulty maintaining a stable self-concept and may experience an identity crisis.

Medication and borderline

Borderline personality disorder (BPD) is a mental illness characterized by instability in emotions, interpersonal relationships, identity and self-image, and impulsive behavior. Appropriate medication can help to reduce the symptoms of BPD and improve the lives of those affected. In this article, we will look at some of the most commonly prescribed medications for borderline patients. Antidepressants Antidepressants are often used to treat BPD as they can help to alleviate symptoms such as anxiety, depression and mood swings. Selective serotonin reuptake inhibitors (SSRIs) are a commonly prescribed type of antidepressant for BPD patients. They work by increasing the availability of serotonin in the brain, a neurotransmitter responsible for stabilizing mood and reducing anxiety and depression. Another commonly prescribed antidepressant for borderline patients are tricyclic antidepressants (TCAs), which also increase the availability of serotonin and noradrenaline. However, TCAs can have serious side effects and are therefore often only a second choice if SSRIs are not effective. Mood stabilizers Mood stabilizers are medications that can help reduce the symptoms of BPD by stabilizing mood and preventing emotional outbursts. Lithium is a commonly prescribed mood stabilizer for borderline patients. It works by regulating the release of neurotransmitters such as serotonin and noradrenaline in the brain. Other mood stabilizers such as valproic acid and lamotrigine are also used in the treatment of BPD. Antipsychotics Antipsychotics are often used in BPD to relieve symptoms such as delusions, hallucinations and paranoia. They can also help to reduce impulsive behavior and mood swings. Atypical antipsychotics such as olanzapine and quetiapine are the most commonly prescribed. These drugs work by affecting the action of dopamine, a neurotransmitter responsible for regulating emotions, in the brain. Anxiety medications Anxiety medications such as benzodiazepines can be prescribed for BPD to relieve anxiety and panic attacks. These drugs work by calming the central nervous system and promoting relaxation. However, benzodiazepines can be addictive and their long-term use can lead to tolerance and withdrawal symptoms.

Borderline and emotion regulation

Borderline personality disorder is a mental illness characterized by unstable moods, interpersonal relationships and self-perception. People with borderline personality disorder often have difficulty regulating their emotions, which can lead to impulsive behavior, self-harm and suicidal thoughts. In this text, I will go into more detail about what emotion regulation is and what specific challenges people with borderline have with it. Emotion regulation refers to the ability to recognize, accept and appropriately regulate emotions. This means being able not only to feel emotions, but also to understand and control them. Emotion regulation is important for maintaining interpersonal relationships, coping with stress and being able to function in everyday life. People with borderline often have difficulties with emotion regulation, which can lead to unstable moods and impulsive behavior. It can be difficult to understand and accept their own emotions, which can lead to conflicts with other people. In addition, their emotional instability can make it difficult for them to cope with stress and strain, which can lead to an increased risk of mental illnesses such as anxiety and depression. There are various strategies and techniques that can help with emotion regulation. These include, for example, breathing exercises, cognitive restructuring and mindfulness meditation. However, people with borderline personality disorder may experience some specific challenges that can make these techniques more difficult. One challenge with emotion regulation in borderline is that emotions are often very intense and rapidly changing. People with borderline can feel happy and content one minute and angry or distressed the next. This can make it difficult to accept and regulate emotions as they change so quickly and are often unpredictable. Another challenge is that people with borderline often have difficulty naming and identifying emotions. They may have difficulty distinguishing between different emotions or expressing their own emotions. This can lead to them feeling lost in their emotions and having difficulty controlling them. Another problem is that people with borderline often have difficulty tolerating negative emotions such as sadness, anger or fear. They may feel overwhelmed and act impulsively to avoid or reduce these emotions. This can lead to self-harm or other self-harming behaviors. Special forms of therapy such as Dialectical Behavioral Therapy (DBT) can help to overcome these challenges in emotion regulation.

Mindfulness and borderline

Borderline personality disorder (BPD) is a complex mental illness that affects the way people regulate their emotions and interact with others. Mindfulness is a practice that can help people to consciously focus on the present moment and reduce negative thoughts and emotions. In this text, I will write 600 words about how mindfulness can help people with borderline personality disorder. People with BPD often have difficulty regulating their emotions and focusing appropriately on interpersonal situations. Mindfulness can help to focus on the present and reduce negative thoughts and emotions. Through mindfulness practices such as meditation, yoga and breathing exercises, people with BPD can learn to control their thoughts and emotions and focus their attention on the present. Mindfulness can also help to reduce the effects of stress on people with BPD. People with BPD are often vulnerable to stress and can suffer from chronic stress, which can lead to a worsening of their symptoms. Mindfulness can help to reduce stress and improve physical and emotional health. Another benefit of mindfulness for BPD is that it can help to break negative thought patterns. People with BPD often have negative thoughts and can feel trapped in a cycle of self-destructive behaviors and emotions. Through mindfulness, they can learn to recognize and interrupt these thoughts and patterns, which can lead to a reduction in their symptoms. Mindfulness can also help to improve the interpersonal relationships of people with BPD. People with BPD often have difficulty focusing on other people and staying in interpersonal relationships. Through mindfulness, they can learn to focus their attention on the present moment and their interpersonal relationships, which can help to improve their relationships. There are many different mindfulness practices that people with BPD can try to reduce their symptoms. Meditation is one of the most popular mindfulness practices, and there are many different types of meditation that people with BPD can try. Body scan meditation, which focuses attention on the different parts of the body, can help to focus on the present moment and reduce negative thoughts and emotions. Yoga is another popular mindfulness practice that people with BPD can try. Yoga can help to relax the body and focus attention on the present moment.

Borderline and interpersonal skills

Borderline personality disorder (BPD) is a mental illness characterized by emotional instability, impulsive behavior, interpersonal difficulties and identity insecurity. Those affected often have difficulty regulating their emotions and can react extremely sensitively to criticism or rejection. In this context, there may be difficulties in dealing with other people, as those affected often exhibit inappropriate behavior in interactions with others. The interpersonal difficulties that can occur with BPD include difficulties in bonding and building relationships. For example, those affected may have difficulty forming or maintaining close relationships. This can lead to them often feeling isolated and lonely. Those affected may also tend to be extremely idealizing or devaluing in relationships. They can also switch quickly between these two extremes. For example, one minute they may idealize their partner and view them as perfect, while the next minute they may feel that they hate them and abandon them. In addition, those with BPD may also have difficulty communicating their own needs and boundaries. They may have difficulty saying no or asking for help when they need it. They may also tend to subordinate their own needs and desires to the needs of others in order to avoid conflict or to avoid being rejected. Another characteristic of BPD is a high sensitivity to rejection or criticism. Those affected can often feel that others reject them or dislike them, even if there are no clear signs of this. They may also tend to see criticism as a personal attack and react to it with anger or sadness. The emotional instability that occurs with BPD can also lead to impulsive behavior. Affected individuals may engage in risky behaviors such as substance abuse, unprotected sex, overeating or gambling. They may also tend to act impulsively and get involved in conflicts or arguments that could be avoided. In terms of treating BPD, various therapeutic approaches can be helpful. One common method is Dialectical Behavioral Therapy (DBT), which aims to improve the emotional regulation skills of those affected and help them cope with interpersonal difficulties. Another form of therapy is schema therapy, which aims to change deeply rooted beliefs and behavioral patterns.

Social support and borderline

Borderline personality disorder (BPD) is a severe mental illness characterized by instability of emotions, relationships and self-image. People with BPD often have difficulty maintaining relationships and frequently experience feelings of emptiness and loneliness. Social support and interpersonal relationships play an important role in coping with the symptoms of BPD. Social support is an important resource that helps people cope with stressful situations and maintain their health. Social support can be offered in the form of emotional support, practical help, information sharing or financial support. People with BPD often find it difficult to maintain stable relationships and can feel lonely and isolated. They may also have difficulty accepting help from others or asking for help. This can cause them to withdraw from others and isolate themselves further. A study by Aviram et al (2006) examined the effects of social support on the symptoms of BPD. The results showed that people with BPD who received more social support had lower symptoms of depression and anxiety. The study also found that the type of social support was important. Emotional support and practical help were most effective in reducing symptoms of BPD. Another study by Dyck et al (2004) examined the effects of social support on the ability of people with BPD to cope with stress. The results showed that people with BPD who had higher levels of social support were better able to cope with stressful situations. The authors concluded that social support plays an important role in coping with stress and can help people with BPD achieve better outcomes. However, it can also be difficult to obtain social support when suffering from BPD. People with BPD may tend to act impulsively or engage in unhealthy relationships.

They may also have difficulty asking for help or accepting support from others. One approach that can help increase social support for people with BPD is to participate in support groups or peer support programs. These programs bring people with similar experiences and challenges together and provide a safe and supportive environment where they can share their feelings and experiences and learn from each other. Overall, social support is an important factor in coping with BPD. The ability to have and maintain strong social support can help alleviate symptoms of the disorder. Borderline and alcohol/drug abuse Borderline and alcohol/drug abuse are two serious mental health issues that often go hand in hand. Borderline personality disorder (BPD) is a mental illness characterized by unstable moods, interpersonal relationships and identity. Alcohol and drug abuse are behaviors that are often used as a coping strategy for emotional problems or stress.

Borderline and Alcohol Abuse

People with BPD often have difficulty regulating their emotions. They can move quickly from one extreme to another and experience intense feelings of anger, sadness, fear or joy. To deal with these emotions, many people with BPD turn to alcohol. Alcohol can temporarily improve mood and reduce feelings of anxiety or sadness. However, some people with BPD may have difficulty controlling their alcohol consumption due to their unstable moods. They can quickly become dependent and drink excessively, which can lead to further emotional problems. People with BPD also often have difficulty stabilizing their relationships with other people. They may act impulsively and get into conflicts, which can lead to social isolation. Alcohol can act as a social lubricant and make it easier to build or maintain relationships. However, due to their impulsive nature, people with BPD can get into risky situations when under the influence of alcohol. They may make careless decisions or get involved in unhealthy relationships, which can further affect their mental health. As with alcohol abuse, substance abuse can be a way for people with BPD to regulate their unstable emotions. Drugs can temporarily improve mood and relieve symptoms of anxiety or depression. Some drugs can also provide a sense of euphoria or strength, which can be very tempting for people with BPD who suffer from low self-awareness or self-esteem. However, substance abuse can also lead to significant physical and psychological problems. Many drugs are addictive and can interfere with the person's life. Some drugs can also lead to psychotic symptoms, such as hallucinations or delusions. People with BPD already have difficulty regulating their emotions and their perception of reality, so substance abuse can only exacerbate these problems.

Borderline and eating disorders

Borderline personality disorder and eating disorders are two serious mental illnesses that often occur together. Borderline personality disorder (BPD) is a disorder characterized by instability in emotional regulation, interpersonal relationships, self-image and behavior. Eating disorders, on the other hand, are a group of mental disorders in which there is a disturbed perception of one's own body and eating behavior. Borderline personality disorder and eating disorders: a common combination It is well known that borderline personality disorder and eating disorders often occur together. In fact, up to 50% of people with BPD also have an eating disorder. There are several reasons why these two disorders so often occur together. One reason is that sufferers of borderline personality disorder often have a disturbed relationship with their bodies. They may have difficulty perceiving and regulating their own emotions, which can lead them to use food as a means of regulating their emotions. People with BPD also often have difficulties with self-image, which can lead them to perceive themselves as unattractive or fat, even if they are of normal weight. Another factor is that eating disorders are often used as a means of coping with emotions. People with eating disorders may use food as a means of controlling their emotions and coping with stress or anxiety. This strategy can help in the short term, but in the long term it can lead to further emotional problems. Types of eating disorders There are different types of eating disorders that are often associated with borderline personality disorder: Anorexia Nervosa: This eating disorder is characterized by an extreme fear of gaining weight and a disturbed perception of one's own body. Those affected often try to reduce their weight through extreme dieting and excessive exercise. Bulimia Nervosa: In this eating disorder, phases of overeating alternate with phases of vomiting or excessive exercise. Those affected often have a disturbed perception of their body and experience feelings of guilt and shame about their eating behavior. Binge eating disorder: This eating disorder involves regular episodes of overeating without vomiting or excessive physical activity. Those affected may have difficulty regulating their emotions and often use food as a means of coping with stress or anxiety. Binge eating with borderline: People with borderline personality disorder may also experience binge eating, which is associated with impaired self-perception and impaired emotion regulation.

Borderline and other mental disorders

Borderline is a personality disorder that is often characterized by instability in mood, behavior and interpersonal relationships. People with borderline often have intense and unstable relationships and mood swings. They may act impulsively and often have difficulty regulating their emotions. Some of the symptoms of Borderline are: Intense and unstable relationships: People with Borderline often have difficulty maintaining stable and healthy relationships. They may become involved in close bonds, but may also quickly become emotionally withdrawn or break off these relationships. Mood swings: People with borderline often have extreme mood swings. They can quickly switch from one extreme emotion to another. Self-harming behavior: Self-harm or suicidal thoughts and attempts are common in people with Borderline. Impulsivity: People with borderline can act impulsively and make risky decisions without considering the consequences. Identity problems: People with Borderline often have difficulty finding their own identity and place in the world. There are many different treatment options for borderline, including psychotherapy, medication and support groups. One of the most effective forms of therapy for borderline is Dialectical Behavioral Therapy (DBT), which was developed specifically for people with borderline and aims to teach them skills to better regulate their emotions and control their behavior. Other mental disorders that are also common include depression, anxiety disorders and bipolar disorder. Depression is a common mental disorder characterized by sadness, hopelessness, fatigue and a lack of interest in activities. There are several forms of depression, including major depression, seasonal affective disorder (SAD) and dysthymia. Treatment for depression often includes psychotherapy and medication. Anxiety disorders are mental illnesses characterized by intense and unreasonable fears. Some of the most common forms of anxiety disorders are generalized anxiety disorder (GAD), panic disorder and social anxiety disorder. Treatment for anxiety disorders often includes psychotherapy, medication and support groups. Bipolar disorders are mood disorders characterized by alternating periods of manic and depressive episodes. Manic episodes are characterized by elevated mood, energy and activity, while depressive episodes are characterized by sadness, hopelessness and a decrease in energy and activity. Treatment for bipolar disorder often includes medication and psychotherapy.

Improving quality of life with borderline

Borderline personality disorder (BPD) is a mental illness characterized by unstable emotions, relationships and identity. Symptoms can vary from person to person, but most people with BPD have difficulty regulating their emotions, often experience intense mood swings and struggle to maintain healthy relationships. Although BPD is often considered difficult to treat, there are ways to improve quality of life and alleviate symptoms. Below are 600 words that can help you improve your quality of life with borderline. "Talk to a professional therapist" Treating BPD usually requires the help of an experienced therapist who specializes in treating this disorder. One form of therapy that has proven to be particularly effective is Dialectical Behavioral Therapy (DBT). With DBT, you can learn to regulate your emotions, build healthy relationships and strengthen your identity. Exercise regularly: Regular exercise is a great way to improve your mood and reduce stress. When you exercise regularly, you release endorphins that make you feel good and help ward off negative thoughts. It is advisable to exercise at least three times a week for at least 30 minutes. Pay attention to your diet: A balanced diet can help improve your mood and alleviate your symptoms. Try to include healthy foods such as whole grains, fruit and vegetables in your diet and reduce your intake of sugary and fatty foods. Practice mindfulness: Mindfulness is a technique that can help you stay in the present moment and observe your thoughts and emotions without evaluating or judging them. Practicing mindfulness can help you regulate your emotions and focus on what is important in your life. Set clear goals: By setting clear and realistic goals, you can focus on something positive and focus on your successes instead of focusing on negative thoughts and emotions. Try to set small goals that are easy to achieve and gradually work towards bigger goals. Avoid alcohol and drugs: Alcohol and drugs can worsen the symptoms of BPD and destabilize your mood. If you have difficulty avoiding alcohol or drugs, seek support from a therapist or support group.

Outlook: Hope for people with borderline

Borderline personality disorder (BPD) is a mental illness characterized by intense emotions, unstable relationships, impulsive behavior and identity disorders. People with BPD often struggle with extreme mood swings, self-harm, suicidal thoughts and severe interpersonal difficulties. The diagnosis can feel like a lifelong sentence, but there is hope for people with BPD. In this outlook, I will discuss some of the positive developments in the treatment of BPD. Dialectical Behavioral Therapy (DBT): DBT is an evidence-based psychotherapy developed specifically for the treatment of BPD. It consists of individual and group sessions in which patients learn to regulate their emotions, control impulsive behavior, and resolve interpersonal conflicts. In recent years, DBT has become increasingly accepted and widespread and is considered the gold standard in the treatment of BPD. Mindfulness-based therapies: Mindfulness-based therapies such as mindfulness meditation and mindfulness-based cognitive therapy (MBCT) have been shown to be effective in treating BPD symptoms. These therapies help patients focus on the present moment and observe their emotions instead of slipping into them. Newer drug treatments: There is an increasing amount of research and development in the area of medication treatments for BPD. New antidepressants, antipsychotics, and mood stabilizers are currently being studied to determine their effectiveness in treating BPD symptoms. Group therapy and peer support: Group therapy and peer support are valuable adjuncts to individual therapy and medication. They offer patients the opportunity to interact with other people who have similar experiences and to learn from each other. Peer support groups such as the National Education Alliance for Borderline Personality Disorder (NEABPD) have grown in importance in recent years and do important work to raise awareness of BPD and provide resources for patients and families. Early intervention: Early intervention in BPD can help prevent or alleviate severe symptoms. Early diagnosis and treatment can help minimize the impact of BPD on the patient's daily life. Therefore, it is important that doctors and therapists focus on the early detection of BPD and provide appropriate treatment.

Imprint

Luna Ludwig
Am Anger 3
06869 Coswig
Germany
Luna-Publishing.de